Princeton University

Princeton Handbook

Devoted to the Interest of Student Activities

Princeton University

Princeton Handbook
Devoted to the Interest of Student Activities

ISBN/EAN: 9783337170516

Printed in Europe, USA, Canada, Australia, Japan

Cover: Foto ©ninafisch / pixelio.de

More available books at **www.hansebooks.com**

THE

PRINCETON
HANDBOOK

DEVOTED TO THE INTEREST
OF STUDENT ACTIVITIES . . .

Copyright 1898

Published by
O. B. STRONG & CO
259 Broadway,
New York.

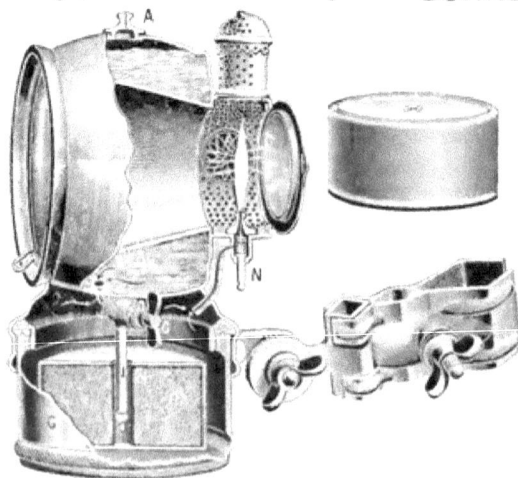

Directory of Officers and Students of Princeton University.

✿ ✿ ✿

NAME	ADDRESS
A. H. Adams,	192 Nassau St.
John Aitken,	9 L P
B. Akin,	17 University Pl.
L. R. Albright,	17 W W
H. M. Alexander,	N. Y. City
J. W. Alexander,	N. Y. City
G. H. V. Allen,	18 N Ed
E. Y. Allen,	18 W W
W. E. Allen,	39 N Ed
W. B. Angle,	11 W W
J. W. Armitage,	6 N R
A. Armstrong, Jr.,	5 S W B
N. B. Armstrong,	5 S W B
H. D. Austin,	57 N Ed
A. C. Ayres,	6 W M W
W. A. Babson,	50 Bayard Ave.
L. J. Bachenheimer,	44 Vandeventer Ave.
R. L. Bachmann Jr.,	9 E B
O. K. Badgley,	29 U P
F. W. Bailey,	4 S E B
J. Baird,	7 U H
J. Baker, Jr.,	17 University Pl.
F. Baker,	9 N M R
J. L. Baldwin,	37 S Ed
J. M. Baldwin,	38 Stockton St.
W. B. Bamford,	1, U H
F. G. Bamman,	15 Dickinson St
C. F. Banks,	5 W B
H. B. Bannard,	F U H
W. H. Bannard,	3 E M W
D. B. Bannerman,	5 S E B
H. C. Barr,	9 U H
R. S. Barr,	4 S W
A. G. Bartholomew,	39 S Ed
L. S. Bartlett,	24 Chambers St.
S. A. Barton,	20 Alex. St.
A. H. Bates,	4 S Ed
C. S. Batt,	32 Wiggins St.
W. H. Batting,	15 University Pl.
J. H. Bawden,	13 N D
G. T. Beacham,	32 Wiggins St.
W. T. M. Beale,	18 E W
V. S. Beam,	3 S Ed
B. Bedford,	8 W B
M. V. Z. Belden,	24 U P
N. D. Belknap,	19 U H
G. R. Bell,	20 U H
H. S. Bennett,	44 Wiggins St.
J. M. Bennett, Jr.,	11 W B
E. N. Benson,	7 N D
R. L. Benson,	51 University Pl.
J. H. Berghans,	53 University Pl.
C. L. Bergland,	63 University Pl.
C. M. Bergland,	62 U H
J. A. Bernhard,	14 S Ed
C. D. F. Bosoré,	22 Dickinson St.
L. L. Biddle,	19 M D
A. D. Bigler,	20 N W
J. H. Bissell,	6 W W
P. A. Bissell,	6 W W
W. H. Black,	44 Vandeventer Ave.
H. C. Blackwell,	8 E B
J. L. Blair,	Blairstown, N. J.
T. D. Blair,	16 S W

NAME	ADDRESS
E. G. Blake,	187 Nassau St.
F. D. Blanchard,	2 S W
A. S. T. Blauvelt,	30 Mercer St.
D. B. Blossom,	21 N Ed
H. A. Boggs,	11 Vandeventer Ave.
W. C. Booth,	13 N M R
S. B. Bope,	2 N W
W. E. Bottger,	10 N R
H. L. Bowlby,	30 S Ed
A. C. Boyd,	7 E B
A. H. Boyd, F.	G, U H
D. Boyd,	10 S M R
J. F. Boyd,	1. P
W. F. Boyd,	7 E B
G. H. Boynton,	31 U H
C. F. Brackett,	4 Prospect Ave.
E. Brady,	24 Edwards Pl.
H. H. Braly,	32 Wiggins St
H. J. Brandt,	10 S K
E. A. Breck,	9 W M W
L. S. Breckinridge,	8 S W B
W. L. Breckinridge,	19 S M R
C. H. Breed,	64 U H
W. M. Brenner,	10 E W
J. R. Brewer,	9 S R
J. Brewer,	39 Nassau St.
F. Briggs,	3 E W
H. C. Briggs,	59 B H (Sem.)
L. R. Brokaw,	128 Nassau St.
A. E. Bronson,	2 M D
J. M. Brooks,	12 W W
J. LeR. Brower,	18 E W
A. Brown,	12 8 W
C. B. Brown,	68 U H
A. H. Brown,	12 N
O. Brown,	73 U H
P. E. Brundage,	10 N
P. N. Bruyere,	11 Vandeventer Ave.
M. G. Buchanan,	S N M R
R. P. Buell,	5 W W
T. N. Bunting,	36 University Pl.
E. W. Burchfield,	23 N Ed
C. L. Burke	Princeton
E. S. Burke, Jr.,	2 U P
C. E. Burr, III,	16 M D
E. P. Burr,	16 M D
L. M. Byrnes,	10 W M W
R. M. Cadwalader, Jr.,	19 M D
A. G. Cameron,	11 Bayard Ave.
H. C. Cameron,	34 Mercer St.
J. R. Campbell,	40 S Ed
T. C. Campbell,	1 M D
S. F. Campbell,	10 S W
W. J. Campbell,	7 N R
G. S. Capelle,	13 W W
R. G. Carew,	11 W W
W. C. Carroll,	41 U H
M. F. Carroll,	3 U H
F. T. Carstensen,	21 S Ed
B. F. Carter,	77 Nassau St.
E. D. Carter,	C E R
H. Carter,	112 Nassau St.
J. B. Carter,	13 N D
N. M. Carter,	16 W W
R. H. A. Carter,	22 Stockton St.

NAME	ADDRESS
R. W. Carter,	N U H
E. T. Casebolt,	11 Dickinson St.
G. H. Casselberry,	K U H
D. L. Chambers,	11 U H
H. M. Chandler,	22 N Ed
H. G. Chatfield,	1 S D
J. H. Chidester,	45 University Pl.
A. De F. Childs,	10 University Pl.
R. Chipman,	3 E M W
E. T. Clark,	23 M D
J. P. Clark,	66 Nassau St.
W. L. Clark, Jr.,	23 U P
E. V. Clausen,	31 University Pl
C. D. Cleghorn,	165 Nassau St.
W. A. Cleland,	9 W B
T. W. Cloney, Jr.,	C U H
J. J. Coale,	30 Mercer St
J. L. Coates,	45 U H
H. J. Cochran,	N U H
F. H. Coffin,	2 E M W
J. T. S. Collier,	10 E W
G. L. Collard,	67 Prospect Ave.
V. L. Collins,	Prin. Bank
J. H. Coney,	164 Nassau St
M. W. Conrow,	109 H. H (Sem.)
W. S. Conrow,	172 Nassau St.
H. P. Converse,	9 W B
J. Converse,	22 M D
D. S. Cook,	7 W M W
H. H. Cook,	Nassau Hotel
G. L. Cooke,	3 L P
O. W. Cooke,	5 N R
R. G. Coolbaugh,	47 Nassau St.
R. Corbin,	60 U H
A. B. Cornwall,	11 N D
H. B. Cornwall,	51 Nassau St
H. S. Cory,	6 N R
T. Cover,	1 U H
H. F. Covington	7 Edwards Pl.
T. O. Cowdrey,	32 Wiggins St.
J. K. Cowen,	Baltimore, Md.
J. Coyle,	22 Vandeventer Ave.
J. E. Crane,	44 Wiggins St.
J. L. Crane,	Princeton Bank
L. B. Crane,	Princeton Bank
E. L. Crawford,	31 University Pl.
J. R. Crawford,	24 Chambers St.
E. R. Craven,	Philadelphia
J. F. Cregan,	10 N R
J. Cromer,	77 U H
R. D. Crow,	4 E M W
E. G. Crowdis,	2 S Ed
E. E. Curtis,	92 Stockton St.
E. Curtis,	12 N M R
U. Dahlgren,	Maple St.
W. P. Dale,	12 E W
R. B. Dalton,	75 U H
H. K. L. Dalzell,	S5 U H
D. T. Dana,	27 University Pl.
H. S. Daniels,	6 W M W
W. M. Daniels,	5 S E B
J. H. Davidson,	58 Nassau St.
J. L. Davis,	7 L P
R. S. Davis,	5 N D
W. H. Davis,	20 S Ed

NAME	ADDRESS
N. W. Dean,	10 U P
J. H. Deane,	110 Nassau St.
H. G. Dechant,	35 N Ed
E. C. Delafield,	9 E B
H. H. Derr,	8 W B
W. H. Detrich,	10 N K
E. D. DeWitt,	1 N D
L. B. DeWitt,	14 U H
J. L. DeWitt,	31 Stedman St.
R. E. Dexter,	5 N M R
L. M. Dickinson,	7 N D
J. R. Dickinson,	5 M D
C. E. S. Dietz,	32 Mercer St.
G. P. Dillenback,	T. U H
E. Dismukes,	12 S M R
J. Dixon,	Trenton, N. J.
A. B. Dod,	2 N D
S. B. Dod, Rev.	Hoboken, N. J.
R. C. Dodd,	26 N Ed
S. W. Dodd,	39 University Pl.
A. Dohm,	106 Nassau St.
K. Donaldson,	7 U H
A. A. Doolittle,	43 U H
F. H. Douglass,	1 U H
H. G. Duffield,	25 University Pl.
J. T. Duffield,	23 University Pl.
C. H. Dugro,	2 Nassau St.
A. V. Duncan,	33 S Ed
A. B. Duvall, Jr.,	9 E M W
W. K. Dwight,	14 S D
A. F. Eastman,	3 Edwards Pl
C. Easton,	12 U Ed
J. B. Edgar,	O. U H
H. J. Edminston,	11 U P
C. F. Edwards,	2 U P
D. L. Edwards,	8 S W
W. H. Edwards,	1 E B
M. O. Edwards,	19 S Ed
G. Eggena,	13 S D
F. P. Ekings,	D. W B
R. Elkins,	35 University Pl.
H. H. Ellison,	11 S D
R. P. Elmer,	4 N M R
J. A. Ely,	6 E W
A. Embury,	172 Nassau St.
C. English,	18 M D
G. K. Erban,	47 University Pl.
E. F. Erdman,	2 S D
W. C. Erdman,	2 S D
H. G. Euwer,	12 N W
J. N. Euwer,	12 N W
J. E. Evans,	27 M D
W. E. Faithorn,	19 University Pl.
J. R. Fan-hawe Jr.,	14 E W
E. W. Farwell,	23 Williams St.
S. S. Feagles,	15 N M R
W. A. Fenstermacher,	29 N Ed
C. Fentress,	21 Dickinson St.
E. F. Ferris,	4 S R
D. F. Filson,	17 S M R
H. B. Fine,	48 Library Pl.
C. B. Finley,	F. U H
V. K. Finley,	39 Nassau St.
J. Fischel,	9 S D
T. W. Fisher,	18 Vandeventer Ave
S. A. Fletcher,	12 U H
W. H. Folk,	9 Park St.
F. W. Ford,	5 W M W
F. W. Fort,	2 S E B
W. Foster, Jr.,	77 Nassau St.
W. S. G. Fowler,	10 U P
N. B. Fox,	5 N W
J. A. Fraser,	11 W B
D. R. Frazer,	Newark, N J.
H. F. Frazer,	60 University Pl.
J. G. Fraser,	29 Vandeventer Ave.
C. V. Freeman,	15 S D
C. K. Fried,	44 Vandeventer Ave.
A. L. Frothingham, Jr.,	Princeton Bank
M. B. Fuller,	12 M D
P. R. Fuller,	5 W M W
W. H. Galarneau,	1 M D
T. F. Galt,	1 W M W
W. G. Gamble,	36 University Pl.
L. S. Gansen,	12 U H
H. E. Gansworth,	42 N Ed
J. C. Gardner,	10 N M R
O. F. Gardner,	34 S Ed
I. Gartner,	39 Nassau St.
F. J. Gay,	53 University Pl.
M. Geer,	4 W M W
W. R. Gelston,	20 Chambers St.
L. George,	79 U H
E. H. Geran,	5 S E B
E. S. Gerhart,	28 N Ed
W. J. T. Getty,	36 N Ed
E. M. Gabby,	104 Nassau St.
J. M. Gidley,	13 N
H. Z. Giffen,	15 U Ed
W. Gillespie,	50 Nassau St.
G. M. Gillette,	41 University Pl.
C. I. Glascow,	36 University Pl.
W. R. Glasgow,	38 U H
E. Glassmeyer,	32 Mercer St.
S. F. Glenn,	14 Edwards Pl.
George Goldie,	35 University Pl.
F. C. Goldsborough,	N E M W
J. Goldsbury,	5 N M R
R. A. Goodenough,	4 N D
G. W. Gordon,	E. W B
J. K. Gordon,	12 S W
P. R. Grace,	51 University Pl.
E. D. Graham,	5 M D
A. W. Granger,	138 Nassau St.
C. B. Gray,	12 S W B
C. S. Gray,	1 N Ed
C. E. Green,	Trenton
E. L. Green,	41 N Ed
W. H. Green,	Princeton
L. A. Greenley,	4 S W
C. Griffin,	2 L P
C. Griswold,	7 U H
L. Griswold,	175 Nassau St.
B. C. Guerin,	7 W M W
L. K. Guiler,	19 N W
H. de H. Gulick,	24 Chambers St.
T. G. Haight,	5 S W
F. J. Hall,	138 Nassau St.
J. Hall,	New York
W. B. Halsey,	11 Dickinson St.
C. L. Hamilton,	4 W M W
S. Hamilton, Jr.,	15 University Pl.
W. S. Hammond,	K. U H
W. A. Harbison,	35 Univ. Pl.
M. L. Harding,	18 S Ed
H. C. Harmon,	9 N R
J. M. Harper,	14 Dickinson St.
M. Harper,	12 Edw H.
W. B. Harris,	36 Mercer St.
J. H. Harrison,	5 N. R
B. Hart,	15 University Pl.
H. M. Hart,	7 S D
C. A. Hastings,	148 Nassau St.
C. A. Hatch,	1 Nassau St.
J. B. Hatcher,	76 Alex. St.
G. R. Hawkins,	19 University Pl.
C. A. Hayden,	17 U H
J. Hayes,	A, L B
E. Headley,	168 Nassau St.
R. Heald,	5 S K
W. E. Hedges,	10 N D
L. Heffelfinger,	14 U H
G. D. Hendrickson,	9 S K
J. A. Henry,	Philadelphia
J. B. Henry,	Philadelphia
C. Herndon,	9 W W
W. E. Heron,	5 N W
J. G. Hibben,	50 Washington St.
F. M. Hill,	10 N
J. H. Hill,	74 U H
A. R. T. Hillebrand,	13 N M R
A. M. Hitlebeitel,	63 U H
E. F. Hiner,	32 N Ed
H. Hipple,	K, U H
W. M. Hitchman,	2 N R
F. B. Hodge,	Wilkesbarre
E. G. Holt,	11 N M K
H. P. Homans,	2 F B
C. E. B. Homer,	24 S Ed
W. E. Hope,	32 N Ed
F. J. Hopper,	32 S Ed
J. F. Hoskins,	Blair Hall
C. H. Howe,	3 S W
W. M. Howell,	148 Nassau St.
C. S. Hudson,	11 Vandeventer Ave.
P. C. Hudson,	112 Nassau St.
M. S. Huey,	30 University Pl.
F. E. Hughes,	26 S Ed
E. F. Hulbert,	1 U H
R. T. Hull,	47 University Pl.
C. L. Humphrey,	1 S L B
W. Humphreys,	Nassau Hotel
B. K. Hunsberger,	25 N Ed
T. W. Hunt,	48 Liberty Pl.
R. A. Hunter,	W. U H
B. G. Huntington,	5 U P
H. C. O. Huss,	47 University Pl.
D. V. Hutchings,	30 U P
J. H. Hutchinson,	20 E W
J. Huvler,	31 University Pl.
R. S. Hyde,	138 Nassau St.
H. Imbrie,	73 U H
J. Imbrie,	192 Nassau St.
M. Imbrie,	192 Nassau St.
F. C. Irish,	19 Vandeventer Ave.
H. F. A. Jackson,	11 F B
M. W. Jacobus,	Hartford, Conn.
J. W. Jameson,	15 Dickinson St.
A. W. Jamieson,	60 University Pl.
F. L. Janeway,	53 University Pl.
J. W. Jarvis,	39 Nassau St.
B. D. Johnson,	4 S R
F. E. S. Johnson,	28 N Ed
K. Johnson,	16 N Ed
C. H. Jones,	70 U H
E. E. Jones,	5 S W
H. L. Jones,	2 Stockton St.
I. Jones,	32 S Ed
L. E. Jones,	16 N W
P. Jones,	Dickinson St.
S. T. D. Jones,	A H (Sem.)
C. S. Judd,	112 Nassau St
F. W. Kates,	C, U H
F. L. Katzenbach,	13 S M R
L. L. Katzenbach,	6 S W B
G. W. Kehr,	5 N Ed
C. R. Kellerman,	23 Ed. Pl.
J. P. Kellogg,	8 L P
O. D. Kellogg,	7 N M R
J. B. Kelly,	192 Nassau St.
M. F. Kelly,	20 W W
E. L. Kendall,	8 M D
J. Kennedy,	27 Williams St.
T. G. Kennedy,	2 W W

PRINCETON FOOT BALL TEAM.

Directory Continued.

NAME	ADDRESS
C. D. Kerr,	19 University Pl.
J. D. Killpatrick,	7 E M W
F. P. King,	2 U P
R. B. Kingsbury,	12 M D
G. B. Kinkead, H.	20 E W
J. S. Kinne,	12 Dickinson St.
J. N. Kinney,	14 M D
L. C. Kleinhans,	79 U H
R. C. Kline,	6 W W
J. Knapp,	21 M D
N. E. Knight,	6 E B
J. W. Knowlton,	1, U H
R. Knox,	2 N R
N. E. Koehle,	19 S M K
M. H. Kratz,	11 N Ed
A. McG. Lane,	138 Nassau St.
C. S. Lane, Jr.,	138 Nassau St.
J. McG. Lane,	66 U H
C. H. Langenberg,	88 Nassau St.
H. H. Langenberg,	88 Nassau St.
R. T. B. Langenberg,	49 U H
G. K. Large,	11 E W
G. H. Lathrope,	2 N D
H. K. Lathrope,	5 M D
H. H. Laughlin,	18 U P
C. S. Lawton,	138 Nassau St.
H. R. Lay,	138 Nassau St.
A. Leake, Jr.,	14 M D
P. Le Boutillier,	5 U P
C. R. Lee,	172 Nassau St.
O. S. Lee,	9 S W
R. A. Lemcke,	15 Dickinson St.
C. Levy,	28 S Ed
A. H. Lewis,	35 U P
E. S. Lewis,	Nassau Hotel
H. B. Lewis,	15 S D
Wm. Libbey,	20 Bayard Ave.
G. H. Light,	9 W W
F. L. Linen,	32 Mercer St.
H. Little,	192 Nassau St.
R. D. Little,	2 E B
F. V. Lloyd,	32 U H
H. Logan,	6 M D
E. H. Loomis,	16 Vandeventer Ave.
S. Q. Loose,	4 W M W
F. D. Lovejoy,	S, U H
E. O. Lovett,	40 Prospect Ave.
W. B. Lydecker,	173 Nassau St.
C. A. Lyon,	20 Vandeventer Ave.
H. E. Lyon,	20 Vandeventer Ave.
A. G. MacConnell,	39 University Pl.
E. O. Mackenzie,	11 N D
J. A. Mackenzie,	3 E B
George Macloskie,	239 Nassau St.
D. Macphee,	S N Ed
W. F. Magie,	58 Library Pl.
W. J. Magie,	Elizabeth, N. J.
G. W. M. Maier,	3 N Ed
J. Maltman,	44 U H
A. Marquand,	Guernsey Hall
A. G. Marr,	24 N Ed
W. Marshall,	S N R
C. Martin, Rev.	342 Nassau St.
H. B. Martin,	6 S K
S. K. Martin, Jr.,	9 E B
W. F. Martin,	9 S E B
D. W. Marvin,	12 S E B
S. B. Mason,	15 Dickinson St.
H. J. Matthews,	U, U H
L. J. Matthews,	30 University Pl.
G. M. Mattis,	138 Nassau St.
J. C. McAtee,	9 S Ed
H. McBride,	77 U H
T. N. McCarter,	Newark, N. J.
J. N. McCaughrin,	88 Nassau St.

NAME	ADDRESS
I. W. McCay,	80 University Pl.
H. McClenahan,	Prospect Ave.
C. A. McClure,	11 N Ed
C. F. McClure,	80 University Pl.
J. J. McCook,	New York
C. H. McCormick,	Chicago
C. B. McCulloh,	14 U H
J. McCurdy, Jr.,	23 Williams St.
S. McDowell,	18 S M R
W. C. McGibbon, Jr.,	3 W M W
C. V. McKaig,	35 University Pl.
W. C. McKee,	40 N Ed
J. T. McKennan,	7 N M K
G. S. McKnight,	39 Nassau St.
G. B. McKinney,	12 S E B
J. C. McLanahan,	2 Nassau St.
W. H. McLauchlin,	168 Nassau St.
J. McLean,	45 University Pl.
J. N. McCleod,	32 Mercer St.
C. McMillan,	40 Bayard Ave.
S. J. McPherson,	Chicago
E. C. McWilliams,	Edwards Pl.
J. M. Williams, Jr.,	47 Univ. Pl.
E. B. Meigs,	30 U H
C. G. Meinken,	39 University Pl.
L. O. Mellinger,	18 Vandeventer Ave.
A. D. Merrick,	25 N Ed
A. Messiter,	S S E B
W. J. Metzger,	O, U H
W. C. Meyers,	41 University Pl.
M. Miles,	27 Chambers St.
W. S. Miles,	4 E B
A. M. Miller,	5 Nassau St.
C. Miller,	1 N Ed
F. D. Miller,	30 N Ed
H Miller,	6 S W B
H. Miller,	51 University Pl.
J. N. Miller,	10 S W B
A. H. Mitchell,	40 Nassau St.
B. B. Mitchell,	192 Nassau St.
H. F. Mitchell,	4 S Ed
E. S. Mitchell,	3 S W B
P. Mitchell,	48 Mercer St.
A. D. Mittendorf,	4 U H
J. H. Moffatt,	G, U H
H. F. Montagnier,	S W W
M. Moody,	5 N D
H. H. Moore,	10 S K
J. E. Moore,	256 Nassau St.
S. Moore,	2 E M W
J. S. Morgan,	cor. Stockton & Elm
J. E. Morris,	15 U P
J. D. Morrow,	60 University Pl.
P. K. Morrow,	2 Nassau St.
C. H. Morton,	9 N K
W. B. Mount,	192 Nassau St.
W. F. Mountain,	40 Nassau St.
H. S. Mudge,	44 Mercer St.
C. H. Murphey,	15 N W
J. O. Murray,	73 Nassau St.
M. S. Murray,	Edwards Pl.
J. F. Neary,	12 U H
F. Neher,	80 University Pl.
W. N. Nevius,	61 W
E. T. Newton,	Sem.
W. C. Nichols,	11 Dickinson St.
E. W. Nicholson,	3 S W B
N. Noble,	15 U P
J. L. Norris, Jr.,	5 S W B
J. H. Northrup,	30 N Ed
G. D. Oberteuffer,	15 U P
H. Z. O'Brien,	16 S M R
G. H. O'Donnell,	6 S E B
H. K. B. Ogle,	30 Mercer St.
C. L. Olds, Jr.,	32 Mercer St.

NAME	ADDRESS
F. G. Olds,	30 Mercer St.
H. R. Omwake,	24 Chambers St.
A. F. Ormond,	109 Alexander St.
S. S. Orris,	66 Nassau St.
A. E. Ortman,	66 Williams St.
E. C. Osborn,	College Offices
C. L. Otis,	6 E B
W. A. Packard,	College H.
S. H. Park,	11 S W
C. Parker,	2 E W
J. M. Parrott,	104 Mercer St.
H. Parsons,	6 E M W
R. S. Parsons,	192 Nassau St.
F. L. Patton,	Prospect
G. S. Patton,	Prospect
W. M. Paxton,	Princeton
W. G. J. Pearson,	22 S Ed
H. H. Pease,	12 M D
G. E. Peebles,	9 E M W
W. M. Peebles,	35 University Pl.
S. H. Pennington,	Newark
B. Perry,	254 Mercer St.
R. B. Petty,	29 Vandeventer Ave.
W. F. Petty,	29 Vandeventer Ave.
E. F. Phelan, Jr.,	172 Nassau St.
A. M. Phillips,	41 Vandeventer Ave.
J. H. B. Phillips,	2 S W
A. H. Pierson,	64 U H
J. R. Pierson,	39 University Pl.
R. E. Pitcairn,	30 Mercer St.
H. L. Pitkin,	23 M D
W. C. Pitkin,	3 W B
E. C. Platt, Jr.,	V, U H
S. H. Plumb, Jr.,	12 Dickinson St.
A. Poe,	5 W M W
G. Poggenburg,	36 University Pl.
W. S. Poindexter,	51 N Ed
A. Pomeroy,	2 M D
R. H. Poole,	10 L P
R. G. Porter,	138 Nassau St.
M. B. Post,	11 S E B
P. C. Prentice,	13 S W
G. M. Priest,	47 University Pl.
G. T. Priest,	11 M K
E. S. Prieth,	12 N M R
W. C. Prinn,	New York
M. T. Pyne,	Princeton
W. D. Quackenbush,	S N K
J G. Ralston,	10 S D
R. Rand,	47 U H
W. M. Rankin,	60 University Pl.
D. B. S. Rathbun,	1 S W B
C. L. Raymond,	85 Bayard Ave.
R. C. Reading,	K, U H
W. F. Redington,	4 S E B
J. V. Redfield,	20 U P
D. A. Reed,	3 N D
G. K. Reed,	2 N W
T. Reed,	cor. Prospect Ave.
H. M. Reeve,	168 Nassau St.
N. S. Reeves,	31 S Ed
E. F. Reichner,	61 U H
L. R. Reid,	47 U H
G. L. Reilly,	3 S D
P. S. Rice,	53 University Pl.
R. H. Rice,	19 University Pl.
G. D. Richards,	28 Chambers St.
E. C. Richardson,	Mercer Heights
J. M. Richardson,	2 S W
C. H. Rickey,	11 N D
B. Ripley,	8 Dickinson St.
L. A. Robb,	15 M D
C. K. Robbins,	13 S Ed
E. V. Robbins,	6 S D
J. H. Robbins,	2 Nassau St.

NAME	ADDRESS
G. F. Roberts,	22 Dickinson St.
T. W. Roberts,	11 S D
C. A. Robinson,	45 University Pl.
H. Robinson,	12 U H
A. B. Robinson,	2 L P
W. M. Robinson,	12 W B
C. G. Rockwood,	34 Bayard Ave.
W. S. Roe,	15 S D
J. L. Rodgers,	13 N Ed
F. T. Root,	86 Nassau St.
W. V. Rosenkrans,	7 S E B
George Ross,	47 U H
P. S. Ross,	39 University Pl.
A. H. Rowan,	2 E B
J. C. Royle,	8 S W B
V. D. Rusling,	15 N M R
G. J. Russell,	17 E W
G. M. Russell,	79 Alexander St.
J. I. Saks,	D, U H
F. W. Salmon,	7 N R
J. B. Sansom,	9 N M R
H. M. Saylor,	33 Vandeventer Ave.
R. Schaff,	39 University Pl.
J. S. Schanck,	18 Nassau St.
H. L. Schenck,	13 S Ed
L. B. Schmidt,	294 Nassau St.
T. S. Schultz,	3 N H
W. M. Schultz,	16 W W
L. Schupp, Jr.,	18 S W
J. P. Schurman,	11 Vandeventer Ave
H. S. Schwarz,	8 E M W
D. C. Scott,	6 S E B
F. H. Scott,	4 E M W
G. C. Scott,	1 S W
S. B. Scott,	15 S M R
W. B. Scott,	56 Bayard Ave.
W. P. Scott,	22 M D
W. P. Seymour,	47 University Pl.
H. E. Shaffer,	40 S Ed
J. S. Sharpe,	S S W
S. H. Shepley,	32 N D
E. C. Sheppard,	3 S M R
C. W. Shields,	Morven
G. J. Siedler,	148 Nassau St.
H. F. Sill,	47 University Pl.
W. J. Slidell,	6 W M W
B. Sloane,	23 M D
J. R. Sloane,	9 S W
A. T. Smith,	G. U H
C. K. Smith,	17 S Ed
H. A. Smith,	3 Witherspoon St.
H. S. S. Smith,	4 E W
L. I. Smith,	40 U H
R. W. Smith,	7 E M W
W. S. Smith,	5 Witherspoon St.
T. S. Snyder,	48 U H
K. H. Southard,	17 E W
H. N. Spencer,	1 W M W
W. W. Staake,	2 E M W
J. N. Steele,	2 Nassau St.
R. S. Steen,	14 University Pl.
J. G. Stevenson,	1 S R
D. B. Stewart,	20 W W
G. B. Stewart,	Harrisburg, Pa.
J. A. Stewart,	New York
R. M. Stoffregen,	2 U H
F. L. Stratton,	34 Vandeventer Ave
L. M. Strayer,	18 S W
H. Street,	14 W W
C. H. Stuart,	76 U H
J. Stuart,	39 U H
H. M. Suter,	5 M D
R. W. Sutton,	44 Vandeventer Ave
C. R. Swain,	11 Dickinson St.
W. H. Swift, Jr.,	172 Nassau St.
R. F. Swigart,	7 N W
R. P. Swofford,	32 Wiggins St.
G. H. Taylor, Jr.,	18 Vandeventer
H. W. Taylor,	14 S M R
J. B. Taylor,	32 Wiggins St.
J B. Taylor, Jr.,	3 S M R
S. W. Taylor, Jr.,	8 S M R
B. R. Terhune,	38 S Ed
W. F. G. Thacher,	1 S W B
L. A. Thomas, Jr.,	31 Williams St.
L. S. Thomas,	18 N W
N. Thomasson, Jr.,	4 L P
A. Thompson,	12 S W B
H. D. Thompson,	80 Univ. Pl
R S Thompson,	Edwards H.
W. H. Thompson,	12 W B
W. W. Titus,	11 N D
J. W. Topley,	32 Wiggins St.
F. C. Torrey,	8 N W
A. N. Turnbull, Jr.,	16 M D
H. N. Twells,	19 S W
W. L. Uyat,	93 Alexander St.
W. L. Upson,	11 E B
L. R. Urban,	15 S E D
W. M, Urban,	27 William St.
C. H. Vail,	9 W B
W. Van Buskirk,	10 N M R
W. M, Vance,	9 L P
H. N. Van Dyke,	College Offices
J. E. Van Dyke,	A E B
J. S. Van Dyke,	10 E M W
J. M. Vincent,	3 N R
A. E. Vandermuhll,	35 Univ. Pl.
K. L. von Krug,	8 S R
G. S. Voorhees,	12 Chambers St.
I. W. Voorhees,	Griggstown, N. J.
S. F. Voorhees,	10 S W
F. C. Voorhies,	110 Nassau St.
P. Vredenberg, H.	3 L P
N. Vreeland,	11 S W B
R. O. Waage,	8 S Ed
F. K. Wainwright,	88 Nassau St.
L. Wallace,	2 Nassau St.
R. A. B. Walsh,	Princeton
H. L. Walton,	144 Nassau St.
F. H. Ward,	6 S E B
J. R. Wardrop,	16 E W
W. M. Wardrop,	16 E W
E. F. Warner, Jr.,	15 Univ. Pl.
G. A. Warren,	3 E B
H. C. Warren,	80 University Pl.
E. C. Wartman,	23 N Ed
W. H. Watkins,	17 W W
H. A. Watres,	32 Mercer St.
S. J. Watson,	4 S R
R. Weber,	N
R. Webster,	12 S D
M. L. Weil,	148 Nassau St.
J. L. Wellington,	41 University Pl.
R. Wentworth,	26 N Ed
A. F. West,	5 Prospect Ave.
E. L. West,	240 Nassau St.
J. H. Westcott,	Mercer Heights
A. S. Weston,	4 S D
H. Wheeler,	19 M D
H. N. White,	32 Wiggins St.
J. A. White,	2 S M R
S. S. White, III,	2 S W B
R. R. Whiting,	15 University Pl.
S. F. Whitman,	43 Vandeventer Ave
G. B. Whitmore,	23 S Ed
J. V. B. Wicoff,	13 S M R
M. C. J. Wichle,	3 S E B
T. F. Wilcox,	7 U P
F. E. Wilkes,	8 N M R
R. Y. Williams,	168 Nassau St.
S. Williamson,	32 N Ed
W. D. Willigerod,	10 U H
H. S. Williston,	32 U P
J. S. Willock,	68 Nassau St.
F. N. Wilson,	Stony Brook
A. L. Wilson,	47 University Pl.
C. H. Wilson,	17 N Ed
E. B. Wilson,	34 Vandeventer Ave.
F. J. Wilson,	7 S W B
J. G. Wilson,	3 E B
J. L. Wilson,	8 W W
S. G. Wilson,	138 Nassau St.
W. Wilson,	50 Library Pl.
S. K. Winans,	58 University Pl.
P. Witherspoon,	69 U H
J. R. Woodcock,	1 S E B
H. R. Wooden,	12 S Ed
F. V. Wooldridge,	12 E B.
E. S. Worcester,	14 N D
A. S. Wright,	50 U H
J. B. Wright,	34 Vandeventer Ave.
W. A. Wyckoff,	27 S Ed
J. Yates,	32 Wiggins St.
C. Yeomans,	70 U H
C. A. Young,	Prospect Ave.
W. G. Young,	30 Mercer St.
W. W. Young,	4 S W B
F. D. Yuengling,	18 U H
G. W. Yuengling,	31 University Pl.
H. S. Zimmerman,	25 S Ed

ABBREVIATIONS.

N.,	Nassau Hall
N. W.,	North Entry of West College
S. W.,	South Entry of West College
N. R.,	North Entry of Reunion Hall
S. R.,	South Entry of Reunion Hall
N. M. R.,	North Middle Entry of Reunion Hall
S. M. R.,	South Middle Entry of Reunion Hall
E. W.,	East Entry of Witherspoon Hall
W. W.,	West Entry of Witherspoon Hall
E. M. W.,	East Middle Entry of Witherspoon Hall
W. M. W.,	West Middle Entry of Witherspoon Hall
U. H.,	University Hall
U. P.,	Upper Pyne Dormitory
N. Ed.,	North Entry of Edwards Hall
S. Ed.,	South Entry of Edwards Hall
N. D.,	North Entry of Albert Dod Hall
M. D.,	Middle Entry of Albert Dod Hall
S. D.,	South Entry of Albert Dod Hall
W. B.,	West Entry of Brown Hall
S. W. B.,	South West Entry of Brown Hall
E. B.,	East Entry of Brown Hall
S. E. B.,	South East Entry of Brown Hall
A. S.,	Alexander Dormitory, Seminary
B. S.,	Brown Dormitory, Seminary
H. S.,	Hodge Dormitory, Seminary
L. P.,	Lower Pyne Dormitory

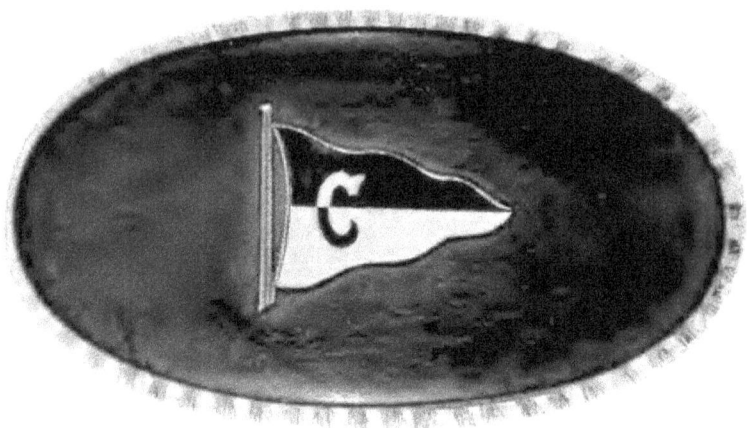

How does this strike you for a Present?
Flag in Silver and Enamel.

Price $10.00 Per Pair.

THE NEATEST COLLEGE BADGE MADE.

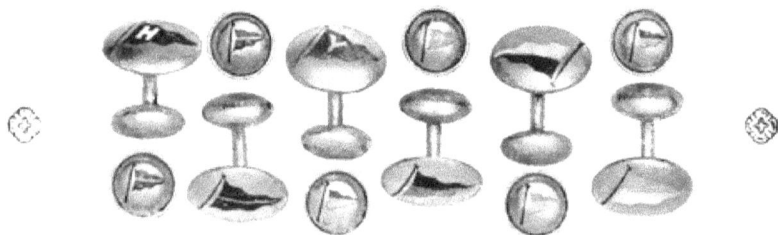

In Sterling Silver and Enamel.

Price $1.50 Per Pair.

O. B. STRONG & Co.,
258 Broadway,
New York.

CHAMPIONSHIP TEAM OF 1897.

Calendar of Princeton University.

For the Fall of 1898.

. . . .

Sept., 20-21	Examinations for admission and the removal of entrance conditions in Princeton only.
Sept. 21	First term begins - College assembles at 3 p.m. in Marquand Chapel.
Sept. 26-Oct. 1	Examinations for removal of first and second term conditions.
Sept. 28	Preliminary examinations for University Degrees.
Oct. 21	Meeting of the Board of Trustees.
Oct. 22	Commemoration Day.
Oct. 31-Nov. 1	Second opportunity for removal of second term conditions.
Nov. 24	Thanksgiving Day.
Dec. 24	12:30 p.m. Christmas vacation begins.

DRAMATIC CLUB.

Ex-President McCosh.

THE McCOSH WALK

Foot Ball,

❧❧❧

DIRECTORS, '96-'97.

W. H. ANDRUS, '97,   Manager.

HARRISON HALL, '98,   Asst. Manager.

GARRETT COCHRAN, '98,   Captain.

DIRECTORS, '97 '98.

HARRISON HALL, '98,   Manager.

DAVID S. COOK, '99,   Ass't Manager.

GARRETT COCHRAN, '98,   Captain.

Average weight of the line,   184½ lbs.

Average weight of the backs,   169½ lbs.

Average weight of the whole team,   177   lbs.

PRINCETON IN THE YALE GAME.

BROKAW, Left End,	Weight, 159	COCHRAN, Right End,	Weight,	162
CHURCH, Left Tackle,	190	SMITH, Quarter,	"	157
CROWDIS, Left Guard,	225	BANNARD, Left Half,		168
GAILEY, Centre,	" 195	KELLY, Right Half,		168
ARMSTRONG, Right Guard,	" 187	BAIRD, Full Back,		153
HILLEBRAND, Right Tackle,	" 174			

FIRST SUBSTITUTES.

THOMPSON, End,	Weight, 158	POE, Quarter, Half,	Weight,	142
TYLER, Tackle,	" 178	BOOTH, Centre, Guard,	"	185
ROSENGARTEN, Half,	164	EDWARDS, Guard,		227
REITER, Half,	" 162	WHEELER, Half, Full Back,		175

FOOT BALL PRACTICE. VARSITY FIELD.

TRACK TEAM.

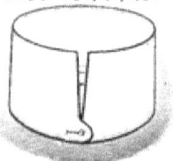

❧ ❧ Princeton Records ❧ ❧

❧ ❧ ❧

EVENT	RECORD	HOLDER
100 Yards Dash,	9⅘ sec.,	L. H. Cary, '93
220 Yards Dash,	22 sec.,	L. H. Cary, '93
440 Yards Dash,	49 sec.,	J. H. Colfelt, '00
120 Yards Hurdle Race,	16⅖ sec.,	H. Wheeler, '00
220 Yards Hurdle Race,	26⅘ sec.,	T. B. Turner, '93
Half Mile Run,	1 min. 57⅗ sec.,	C. H. Kilpatrick, '99
One Mile Run,	4 min. 26 sec.,	J. Cregan, '99
One Mile Walk,	6 min. 54½ sec.,	F. A. Borcherling, '95
Two Mile Bicycle Race,	5 min. 29⅘ sec.,	J. B. Corser, '96
Freshman 440 Yards Dash,	52 sec.,	Goldthwaite, '99
Running High Jump,	6 ft. ½ in.,	W. C. Carroll, '00
Running Broad Jump,	22 ft. 5 in.,	R. C. Kumler, '95
Pole Vault,	10 ft. 10 in.,	A. C. Tyler, '97
Putting 16-Pound Shot,	41 ft. 10¾ in.,	R. Garrett, Jr., '97
Throwing 16-Pound Hammer,	124 ft. 5 in.	H. C. Potter, '98
Indoor High Jump,	5 ft. 11 in.,	W. C. Carroll, '00
Springboard Jump,	8 ft. 10 in.,	E. S. Ramsdell, '94
Indoor Pole Vault,	10 ft.,	A. C. Tyler, '97

Eighth Annual Open Handicap Games of the Princeton University Track Athletic Association

✦✦✦

At the University Grounds, May 1, 1897.

EVENTS	WINNERS	TIME, HEIGHT OR DISTANCE
100 Yards Dash,	Wills, Lawrenceville, 10 yards, Gantz, Princeton Seminary, 9 yards Byers, Yale, 3 yards	9⅗ sec.
120 Yards Hurdle Race,	Clark, B. A. A. and Harvard, 9 yards, Van Buren, Yale, 3 yards McKibben, University of Pennsylvania, 8 yards	16 sec.
One Mile Walk,	Price, University of Pennsylvania, 60 sec., . 7 min. 35½ sec. Worth, University of Pennsylvania, 60 sec. Adams, Yale, 60 sec.	
880 Yards Run,	Cregan, Princeton, 8 yards, . . . 2 min. 2½ sec. Harrison, University of Pennsylvania, 30 yards Steele, University of Pennsylvania, 25 yards	
Two Mile Bicycle Race,	Hill, Yale, 20 yards, . 4 min. 58 sec. Hubbert, Swarthmore, 60 yards McGuire, Columbia, 170 yards	
440 Yards Run,	Sensenig, Haverford, 45 yards, Rodney, Haverford, 40 yards Robb, Princeton, 35 yards	48 sec.
220 Yards Dash,	Wills, Lawrenceville, 18 yards, . . . 22⅖ sec. Quinlan, Fordham, and N. Y. A. C., 4 yards Chappelle, Yale, 6 yards	
220 Yards Hurdle,	Van Ingen, Yale, 3 yards, . . 24⅖ sec. Perkins, Yale, scratch Bijur, Columbia, scratch	
One Mile Run,	Palmer, Princeton, 60 yards, . 4 min. 44½ sec. Paret, Drexel Institute, 65 yards Ross, Haverford, 95 yards	
Putting 16-lb. Shot,	Potter, Princeton, 8 feet, . . . 42 ft. 5 in McCracken, University of Pennsylvania, 3 feet, 42 ft. 3 in Richards, Lawrenceville, 8 feet, . . 41 ft. 5 in	

Handicap Games - Continued

.*.*.*

EVENTS	WINNERS	TIME, HEIGHT OR DISTANCE
Pole Vault,	Tyler, Princeton, scratch,	10 ft. 3½ in.
	Strayer, Princeton, 10 inches,	10 ft. 2½ in.
	Dudley, Lawrenceville, 6 inches,	9 ft. 10 in.
Running Broad Jump,	Mason, Columbia, 22 inches,	24 ft. 9½ in.
	Cowperthwait, Columbia, 15 inches,	24 ft. 8 in.
	Bottger, Princeton, scratch,	24 ft.
Throwing the Discus,	Garrett, Princeton,	100 ft. 11 in.
	Wilson, Princeton,	100 ft.
	Potter, Princeton,	92 ft. 8 in.
Throwing 16-lb. Hammer,	Clark, B. A. A. and Harvard, 30 feet,	144 ft. 5 in.
	McCracken, University of Pa., 21 ft. 7 inches,	144 ft. 2 in.
	Craig, Princeton, 35 feet 9 inches,	143 ft. 4½ in.
Running High Jump,	Dudley, Lawrenceville, 7 inches,	6 ft. 3 in.
	Conklin, Haverford, 3 inches,	6 ft. 4 in.
	Windsor, University of Penn., scratch,	6 ft

.*.*.*

.*.* Summary .*.*

.*.*.*

Princeton,	35 points	Haverford,	10 points
Yale,	17 "	Columbia,	4 "
Lawrenceville,	17 "	Swarthmore,	2 "
University of Pennsylvania,	16 "	Fordham,	2 "
Harvard,	10 "	Drexel Institute,	2 "

We confine ourselves
exclusively to high grade work
in these lines.........

T. F. NEWMAN.

Manufacturer and Designer

COLLEGE FRATERNITY BADGES
SOCIETY & CLASS PINS
MEDALS. &c.

The Wearers of the "C"

Ellis Leeds Aldrich, '97	- -	'Varsity Baseball Team, '95-96.
Theodore Layton Bailey, '99	- -	'Varsity Crew, '97.
Abram Bassford, Jr., '98	- -	'Varsity Baseball Team, '95-96, 'Varsity Football Team, '97.
Wilton Bentley, '98	- -	'Varsity Crew, '95-97.
Charles Hildreth Blair, Jr., '98	- -	'Varsity Baseball Team, '96-97.
Joseph Kirkpatrick Bole, 1900	- -	'Varsity Baseball Team, '97.
Frederick Adams Briggs, '98	- -	'Varsity Crew, '96-97.
Ernest Miller Bull,	-	'Varsity Track Team, '95.
Frank Kenneth Cameron, G.	-	'Varsity Lacrosse Team, '95.
Emmett Browning Carter, '99	-	'Varsity Crew, '97.
Frederick Diamond Colson, '97	-	'Varsity Crew, '95, '96, '97; Captain, '98.
William Cox Dalzell, Jr., '99	- -	'Varsity Crew, '97.
Robert Deming, 1900	-	'Varsity Track Team, '97.
John Joseph Dempsey, '98	-	'Varsity Football Team, '97.
Mark Ray Faville, 1901	- -	'Varsity Football Team, '97.
Schuyler Lyon Fisher, '00	-	'Varsity Crew, '97.
James Henry Gannon, Jr., '98	-	'Varsity Baseball Team, '96.
John Ernest Gignaux, '98	-	'Varsity Track Team, '95, '96, '97
Charles Frederick Hackett, '98		'Varsity Football Team, '97.
Harvey Harrison Haskell, '98	- -	'Varsity Baseball Team, '96-97.
Edgar Johnston, '98	- -	'Varsity Crew, '96.
William V. Kelly, G.		'Varsity Track Team, '95; Lacrosse, '97; Football, '94.
Asa Carlton King, '00	-	'Varsity Crew, '97.
Harold Lee, '97	-	'Varsity Football Team, '97.
Isaac Cook Ludlam, '98		'Varsity Crew, '96.
Archie Byron Lueder, '99	- -	'Varsity Football Team, '96-97.

The Wearers of the "C"—Continued.

WILLIAM MCKEEVER, '98	Captain 'Varsity Football Team, '97
DANIEL MAURER MCLAUGHLIN, '98	Captain 'Varsity Football Team, '98
WILLIAM RAYMOND MILLER, '98	'Varsity Football Team, '96; 'Varsity Baseball Team, '96-97.
CLARENCE STANTON MOORE, '98	'Varsity Crew, '96-97.
JOHN FRANCIS MURTAUGH, '98	'Varsity Baseball Team, '97
CLARENCE MEIGS ODDIE, '99	'Varsity Crew, '97.
MARK M. ODELL, '97	'Varsity Crew, '97.
JOHN QUINCY PERRY, '98	'Varsity Baseball Team, '96
CHARLES UNDERHILL POWELL, '98	Captain 'Varsity Track Team, '98
BENJAMIN POWELL, '96	'Varsity Lacrosse Team, '95.
ROBERT HARRIS RIPLEY, '98	'Varsity Football Team, '96
EDWARD JOSIAH SAVAGE, '98	'Varsity Crew, '96-97.
OLIVER SHANTZ, '91	'Varsity Lacrosse Team, '91.
WILLIAM BOYD STAMFORD, '99	'Varsity Crew, '97
EDWIN REGUR SWEETLAND, '99	'Varsity Football Team, '95
JOSEPH SPRINGER SWINDELLS, '95	'Varsity Lacrosse Team, '95.
CORNELIUS HOAGLAND TANGEMAN, 1901	'Varsity Football Team, '97.
HARRY LEROY TAYLOR, '98	'Varsity Track Team.
WILLIAM HARGADINE THOMPSON, '98	'Varsity Track Team.
LYNDON SANDFORD TRACY, '98	'Varsity Football Team, '96-98.
ALLEN EDWARD WHITING, '98	'Varsity Football Team, '97.
WILLIAM TRUMAN YALE, '97	'Varsity Track Team, '95.
CHARLES VAN PATTEN YOUNG, '99	Captain 'Varsity Baseball Team, '97; 'Varsity Football Team, '96-97.
EUGENE CHARLES ZELLER, 99	'Varsity Track Team, '96.

AROUND ITHACA.

CORNELL 'VARSITY CREW, '98.

NAVAL RECORD

DATE.	OPPONENTS.	WINNER.	TIME.	MILES.	PLACE.
July, 1873.....	Y., H., Wes., A., Col., D., B., T., W., M. A.	Yale..........	16.59	3	Springfield.
July, 1874.......	Col., Wes., H., W., D., T., Y.....	Columbia	16.42	3	Saratoga.
July, 1875......	Col., H., D., Wes., Y., A., Br., W., B., Ham., U. P.	Cornell	16.53½	3	Saratoga.
July, 1879......	H., Col., U., Wes., P.....	Cornell.........	17.01¼	3	Saratoga.
July, 1879......	Col., Wes.............	Columbia.......	8.26	1½	Lake George.
July, 1880......	Col., Penn..............	Cornell.........	9.12	1½	Lake George.
July, 1881......	Hertford	......		1½	Henley.
July, 1882......	Penn., Wes., P., B........	Pennsylvania	9.35	1½	Lake George.
July, 1883......	Penn., P., Wes.........	Cornell.........	11.57	1½	Lake George.
June, 1884......	Penn., P..............	Penn!	9.06½	1½	Philadelphia.
July, 1884......	Penn., Col., P., B.......	Penn!	8.39	1½	Saratoga.
June, 1885......	Penn	Cornell.........	8.38	1½	Philadelphia.
July, 1885......	Br., B., Penn..........	*	9.10½	1½	Worcester.
July, 1887......	B	Cornell.........	9.38¼	1½	Worcester.
July, 1887......	Penn	Cornell.........	8		Philadelphia.
June, 1889......	Col., Penn	Cornell.........	15.30	3	New London.
July, 1889......	Penn	Cornell.........	6.40	1½	Philadelphia.
June, 1890......	B	Cornell.........	17.30	3	Ithaca.
June, 1890......	Penn	Cornell.........	14.43	3	New London.
June, 1891......	Penn., Col............	Cornell.........	14.27½½	3	New London.
June, 1892......	Penn	Cornell.........	17.26	3	Ithaca.
July, 1893......	Penn	Cornell.........	17.26	4	Lake Minnetonka.
June, 1894......	Penn	Cornell.......	21.12	4	Torresdale.
June, 1895......	Col., Penn., *	Columbia	21.25	4	Poughkeepsie.
July, 1895.	Trinity Hall..	Trinity Hall	7.15	7-15	Henley.
June, 1896......	H., Penn., Col........	Cornell	19.20**	4	Poughkeepsie.
June, 1897......	H., Y...............	Cornell........	.....	4	Poughkeepsie.
July, 1897......	Penn., Col...........	Cornell.........	.....	4	Poughkeepsie.
June, 1898......	H., Y...............	Cornell.........	.....	4	New London.
July, 1898......	Penn., Col., Wis	Penn..........	.....	4	Saratoga.

A.—Amherst.
B.—Bowdoin.
Br.—Brown.
C.—Columbia.

D—Dartmouth
H —Harvard.
Ham.—Hamilton.
P.—Princeton.

Penn.—Pennsylvania.
T.—Trinity.
U —Union.
W.—Williams.

Y —Yale.
M. A.—Massachusetts Agricultural College.

! Cornell second.
* Cornell finished first; ruled out on foul.
§ Penn. did not start; Cornell rowed.
: World's record
** American record

April 14......	Cornell 4	Rochester...... 5
" 16....	Cornell...... 7	Rochester......12
" 19.....	Syracuse—Cornell,	Rain.
" 20... ..	Cornell...... 1	Syracuse League 4
" 23.....	Lehigh at Ithaca.	Rain.
" 29.....	Cornell...... 5	Vermont...... 0
" 30	Cornell...... 0	Princeton..... 3
May 4	Cornell...... 6	Syracuse 4
" 7	Cornell...... 8	Harvard...... 5
" 11.....	Cornell...... 5	Lafayette...... 4
" 14	Cornell...... 0	Pennsylvania... 2
" 21.....	Cornell 6	Princeton 11
" 24	Cornell 13	Syracuse....... 9
" 29.....	Cornell...... 3	Pennsylvania... 7
" 30	Cornell...... 8	Columbia 4
June 1	Cornell..... 1	Pennsylvania.... 3
" 4	Williams. . 8	Cornell........ 4
" 11	Lafayette. ..11	Cornell....... 8

.⸟. .⸟. .⸟.

FOOT BALL RECORD.

For 1897.

DATE		SCORE.	OPPONENTS.	SCORE.	PLACE.
Sept. 25th......	Cornell........	6	Colgate	0	Ithaca.
Oct. 2d......	Cornell	10	Syracuse.......	0	Ithaca.
Oct. 9th......	Cornell.........	15	Tufts ,................. ...	0	Ithaca.
Oct. 16th......	Cornell.....	2	Lafayette	4	Easton.
Oct. 23d	Cornell........	0	Princeton..................	10	Ithaca.
Oct. 30th	Cornell.........	5	Harvard	24	Cambridge.
Nov. 6th......	Cornell ,......	45	Penn. State..............	0	Ithaca.
Nov. 13th	Cornell........	42	Williams	0	Buffalo.
Nov. 25th	Cornell....	0	Pennsylvania	4	Philadelphia.

SUMMARY: Games won, 5: Games lost, 3: Tie, 1.

CORNELL CROSS COUNTRY CLUB.

CORNELL ATHLETIC RECORDS

Outdoor.

EVENT.	RECORD.	DATE.	HOLDER.
100-yard dash..................	10 1-5 sec.	May 13, 1892 ... / Oct. 22, 1892 ... / May 9, 1896 ...	F. W. Kane. / W. P. Belknap. / J. R. Bowen.
220-yard dash..................	22 2-5 sec.	May 9, 1896....	H. L. Daniels.
440-yard run	51 2-5 sec.	May 9, 1896....	H. L. Taylor.
880-yard run..................	2 min. 4 2-5 sec.	May 13, 1893 ...	G. W. Kulison.
One-mile run	4 min. 49 sec.	May 13, 1893....	E. P. Andrews.
One-mile walk..................	7 min. 29 2-5 sec.	May 13, 1894....	I. Stern.
120-yard hurdle................	16 4-5 sec.	May 13, 1893...	J. R. Whittemore.
220-yard hurdle................	27 sec.	May 9, 1896...	P. M. Walter.
Two-mile bicycle...............	5 min. 13 sec.	May 13, 1894 ...	E. B. Gorby.
Running high jump	6 ft. 3 8 in.	Oct. 31, 1896....	C. C. Powell.
Running broad jump...........	20 ft. 6 in.	May 7, 1892 ...	A. H. Place.
Pole vault	9 ft. 7 3-8 in.	Oct. 31, 1896...	F. I. Hall.
Putting 16-pound shot....	35 ft. 3 in.	Oct. 22, 1892 ...	J. W. Taylor.
Throwing 16-pound hammer......	123 ft. 2 in.	May 13, 1894 ...	G. L. Patterson.

Indoor.

EVENT.	RECORD.	DATE.	HOLDER.
One-mile walk.............	7 min. 26 3-4 sec.	March 7, 1891	O. Payne.
Running high jump	5 ft. 11 in.	March 6, 1896...	C. C. Powell.
Standing high jump.............	4 ft. 9 7-8 in.	March 5, 1897	I. Burnett.
Standing high kick.............	7 ft. 7 1-2 in.	March 3, 1892 ..	H. G. Reid.
Running high kick......	9 ft. 1-4 in.	March 5, 1893 ...	C. E. Murphy.
Putting 16-pound shot...	39 ft. 2 in.	March 5, 1897...	E. C. White.
Pole vault.....................	9 ft. 7 1-4 in.	March 5, 1897....	J. G. Rosenburg.
Standing broad jump............	10 ft. 6 in.	March 5, 1897....	I. Burnett.

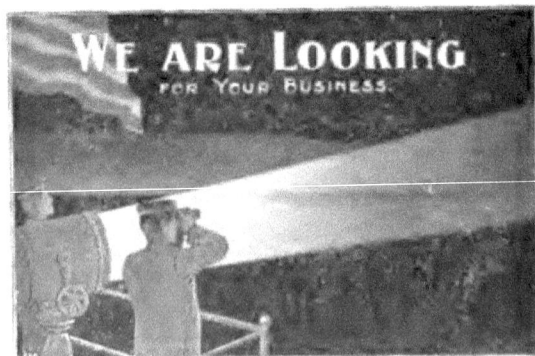

Intercollegiate Records.

✒ ✒ ✒

RACES	NAMES.	TIME.	COLLEGE.
100-yard run	B. J. Wefers	9-⅘ seconds	Georgetown
120-yard hurdle	A. C. Kraenzlein	15-⅖ "	U. of P.
Quarter-mile run	G. B. Shattuck	49-⅘ "	Amherst
Half-mile run	E. Hollister	1 minute 56-⅖ seconds	Harvard
One-mile run	G. W. Orton	4 " 23-⅖ "	U. of P.
One-mile walk	W. B. Fetherman, Jr.	6 " 45-⅖ "	U. of P.
220-yard hurdle	A. C. Kraenzlein	23-⅘ seconds	U. of P.
220-yard run	B. J. Orfers	21-⅘ "	Georgetown
Running broad jump	Myer Prinstein	23 feet 7-⅜ inches	Syracuse
Running high jump	J. D. Winsor, Jr.	6 " 3 "	U. of P.
Putting 16 pound shot	W. O. Hickok	42 " 11-¼ "	Yale
Throwing 16 pound hammer	J. C. McCracken	149 " 5 "	U. of P.
Pole Vault	W. W. Hoyt and G. S. Clapp	11 " 4-⅜ "	Harvard-Yale
Quarter-mile bicycle race	J. F. Williams, Jr.-H. K. Bird	32-⅖ seconds	Columbia
Half-mile bicycle race	G. Ruppert	1 minute 16-⅗ seconds	Columbia
One-mile bicycle race	Ray Dawson	2 " 13-⅖ "	Columbia
Five-mile bicycle race	Ray Dawson	11 " 50-⅖ "	Columbia
One-mile tandem bicycle race	Ray Dawson and J. A. Powell	2 " 10-⅖ "	Columbia

---

Intercollegiate Games of '98.

Winners of '98 Meeting.

Events	U. of Pa.	Princeton.	Harvard.	Yale.	Syracuse.	John Hopkins.	Columbia.	Williams.	Cornell.	Georgetown.
120 hurdle	6	..	2	3	..	..			..	..
100-dash	5	3	2	..	1	..			..	..
440-run	.	5	1	2	3	..			..	..
One-mile run	3	5	2	1	..	..			..	..
One-mile walk	5	..	..	4	..	2			..	..
220 hurdle	5	..	6	..	..				..	..
One-half mile run	..	5	2	1	..			3	..	..
220-dash	7	3	1	..	..				..	..
Throwing hammer	7	3	..	1	..				..	..
Running high jump	2¼	..	..	5¼	..				2¼	..
Pole vault	..	..	3½	7½	..	..			..	..
Running broad jump	5	..	1	..	5				..	..
Putting shot	5	..	..	2	..	3			..	..
Bicycle events	..	3	..	1	..	..	5		..	2
Totals	50⅛	28	25½	22¼	9	5	5	1	2⅛	2

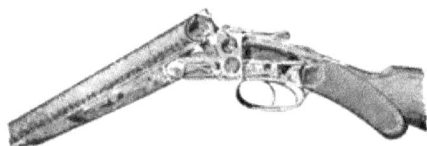

Winners In Previous Years.

Colleges.	1st Prizes.	2d Prizes.	3d Prizes.	Total Points.
Harvard	80	81¼	40 1/12	602 7/12
Yale	68½	63¾	21 5/12	494 5/12
Columbia	55½	50½	15⅓	393⅚
University of Pennsylvania	40	29	16½	279½
Princeton	38	37¼	10 7/12	275 1/12
Dartmouth	5	5	0	35
C. C. N. Y.	3	8	3	34
Amherst	5	4	1	34
Layfayette	4	4	0	28
Wesleyan	4	1	⅓	22⅓
Williams	2	4	⅓	18⅓
Georgetown	3	1	0	17
Cornell	0	3	4⅓	10⅓
Stevens	2	0	0	10
Boston University	2	0	0	10
Union	1	2	0	9
Brown	0	4	⅓	8⅓
Swarthmore	1	0	3	8
University of California	0	2	3	7
University of Michigan	1	0	0	5
Bowdoin	0	1	0	2
Hobart	0	1	0	2
Lehigh	0	0	1	1
Washington and Jefferson	0	0	1	1
Syracuse	0	0	1	1
Trinity	0	¼	¼	¾
Columbian	0	0	½	⅝

Foot Ball Season, '98.

Yale.

Dates.	Played at.	Opponents.	Yale.	Opp.
Sept. 21	Hartford	Trinity	18	0
Oct. 1	New Haven	Wesleyan	5	0
Oct. 5	"	Amherst	34	0
Oct. 8	"	Williams	23	0
Oct. 15	"	Newtown, A. A		
Oct. 19	"	Brown		
Oct. 22	"	Carlisle Indians		
Oct. 29	"	West Point		
Oct. 12	Princeton	Princeton		
Oct. 19	New Haven	Harvard		

.✈. .✈. .✈.

Harvard.

Dates.	Played at	Opponents.	Harvard.	Opp.
Oct. 1	Cambridge	Williams	11	0
Oct. 5	"	Bowdoin	23	6
Oct. 8	"	Dartmouth	21	0
Oct. 12	"	Amherst		
Oct. 15	West Point	West Point		
Oct. 19	Cambridge	Newtown A. A.		
Oct. 22	"	Chicago A. A.		
Oct. 29	"	Carlisle, Ind.		
Nov. 5	"	University of Penna		
Nov. 12	"	Brown		
Nov. 19	New Haven	Yale		

.✈. .✈. .✈.

Princeton.

Dates.	Played at	Opponents.	Princeton.	Opp.
Oct. 1	Princeton	Lehigh	21	0
Oct. 5	"	Stevens	42	0
Oct. 8	"	Franklin and Marshal	58	0
Oct. 12	"	Lafayette		
Oct. 14	Baltimore	Maryland A. C.		
Oct. 15	Annapolis	Naval Academy		
Oct. 22	Princeton	Cornell		
Oct. 26	"	Penn. State College		
Oct. 29	Providence	Brown		
Nov. 2	Princeton	University of Virginia		
Nov. 5	"	West Point		
Nov. 12	"	Yale		

University of Pennsylvania

Dates.	Played at.	Opponents.	U. of P.	Opp.
Sept. 21	Philadelphia	Franklin and Marshal	41	0
Sept. 28	"	Gettysburg	50	0
Oct. 1	"	Penn. State College	40	0
Oct. 5	"	Normal School	50	0
Oct. 8	"	Brown	18	0
Oct. 12	"	University of Virginia		
Oct. 15	"	Lehigh		
Oct. 19	"	Wesleyan		
Oct. 22	"	Lafayette		
Oct. 29	"	University of Chicago		
Nov. 5	Cambridge	Harvard		
Nov. 12	Philadelphia	Carlisle, Ind.		
Nov. 24	"	Cornell		

Cornell.

Dates.	Played At.	Opponents.	Cornell.	Opp.
Sept. 21	Ithaca	Syracuse	28	0
Sept. 24	"	Colgate	28	5
Sept. 28	"	Hamilton	41	0
Oct. 1	"	Trinity	17	0
Oct. 5	Syracuse	Syracuse	18	0
Oct. 8	Ithaca	Carlisle Indian School	23	6
Oct. 15	"	Rochester		
Oct. 22	Princeton	Princeton		
Oct. 29	Ithaca	Oberlin		
Nov. 5	Buffalo	Williams		
Nov. 12	Ithaca	Lafayette		
Nov. 19		No game		
Nov. 24	Philadelphia	Pennsylvania		

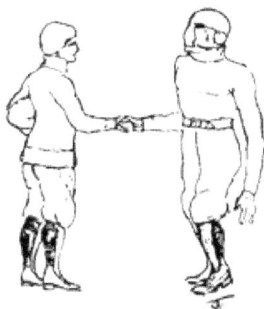

Base Ball Season. '98.

Yale.

Date	Played at	Opponents	Y'e.	Op.
March 30	New Haven	Holy Cross	6	4
April 2	"	Wesleyan	12	4
" 6	New York	Manhat. College	3	10
" 7	Washington	Georgetown	5	2
" 12	"	"	0	6
" 16	New Haven	Springfield	7	4
" 20	"	Williams	12	3
" 23	Amherst	Amherst	6	3
" 27	New Haven	Brown	9	3
May 4	"	Lafayette	0	3
" 7	"	Dartmouth	2	0
" 12	"	Wesleyan	14	13
" 14	Providence	Brown	2	17
May 16	New Haven	U. of Va	2	4
" 19	"	Columbia	23	1
" 27	Newtown	Newtown A. A.	9	8
" 28	Andover	Andover	7	6
" 30	Providence	Brown	3	4
June 4	New Haven	Princeton	7	12
" 8	"	U. of Vt	10	7
" 11	Princeton	Princeton	6	4
" 18	New York	Princeton	8	3
" 23	Cambridge	Harvard	4	9
" 28	New Haven	"	7	0
July 2	New York	"	3	1

❧ ❧ ❧

Princeton.

Date	Played at	Opponents	P'n.	Op.
March 30	Princeton	Fordham	16	8
April 2	Princeton	Columbia	8	3
" 7	Baltimore	Baltimore N. C.	7	9
" 9	Washington	Georgetown	8	5
" 11	"	"	9	2
" 16	Princeton	Franklin and M.	22	1
" 20	"	Lafayette	6	2
" 21	"	Mercersburg	7	5
" 23	New York	Forfeit, Columbus	0	9
" 27	Princeton	Maryland	14	3
" 30	Ithaca	Cornell	3	0
May 4	Princeton	Lehigh	6	1
" 7	"	Brown	6	7
May 12	Princeton	U. of Va	12	5
" 14	"	Harvard	12	2
" 18	Easton	Lafayette	3	7
" 21	Princeton	Cornell	11	6
" 25	"	Brown	4	1
" 28	Cambridge	Harvard	9	2
June 1	Princeton	Georgetown	14	3
" 3	"	Andover	2	9
" 4	New Haven	Yale	12	7
" 8	Princeton	Lawrenceville	10	3
" 11	Princeton	Yale	4	6
" 18	New York	Yale	3	8

❧ ❧ ❧

Harvard.

Date	Played at	Opponents	H'v'd.	Op.
April 7	Cambridge	Cambridge	25	2
" 9	"	Tufts	3	7
" 12	"	Woven Hose	25	1
" 16	N. Caroline	U. of N. C.	10	10
" 18	Virginia	U. of Va	7	5
" 19	Washington	Catholic Union	16	3
" 20	"	Georgetown	1	3
" 22	New York	Columbia	7	2
" 27	Cambridge	Dartmouth	13	7
" 30	Williamsto'n	Williams	22	2
May 2	Andover	Andover	2	1
" 3	Cambridge	Lafayette	1	8
" 7	Ithaca	Cornell	5	8
" 10	Cambridge	Amherst	20	6
" 14	Princeton	Princeton	2	12
May 18	Cambridge	Exters	8	0
" 20	New York	Fordham	9	0
" 21	Philadelphia	U. of Pa	2	3
" 28	Cambridge	Princeton	2	9
June 1	Amherst	Amherst	11	3
" 7	Worcester	Holy Cross	9	4
" 8	Cambridge	Brown	1	5
" 9	"	Graduates	6	4
" 11	"	U. of Pa	2	1
" 15	Providence	Brown	14	3
" 18	Cambridge	Holy Cross	12	5
" 23	"	Yale	9	4
" 28	New Haven	Yale	0	7
July 2	New York	Yale	1	3

University of Pennsylvania.

Dates.	Played at.	Opponents.	U. of Pa.	Opp.
April 2	Philadelphia	Carlisle, Ind.	5	2
" 13	Washington	Georgetown	12	2
" 20	Philadelphia	Manhattan	2	3
" 23	"	Penn. State College	16	0
" 27	"	Lehigh	12	5
" 30	New York	Columbia	3	0
May 7	Philadelphia	Georgetown	2	1
" 11	"	University of Virginia	9	3
" 14	"	Cornell	2	0
" 18	"	Brown	3	2
" 21	"	Harvard	3	2
" 25	"	Lafayette	7	1
" 28	Ithaca	Cornell	7	4
" 30	South Bethlem	Lehigh	3	2
June 1	Philadelphia	Cornell	3	1
" 4	Easton	Lafayette	8	11
" 10	Worcester	Holy Cross	3	11
" 11	Cambridge	Harvard	1	2
" 13	Providence	Brown	0	16

* * *

Cornell.

Dates.	Played at	Opponents.	Cornell.	Opp.
April 13	Ithaca	Rochester	1	5
" 20	"	Syracuse	1	4
" 27	"	"	7	2
" 28	"	University of Vermont	5	9
" 30	"	Princeton	0	3
May 4	"	University of Syracuse	6	4
" 7	"	Harvard	8	5
" 11	Easton	Lafayette	5	4
" 12	Orange	Orange A. C.	1	9
" 14	Philadelphia	University of Pennsylvania	0	2
" 21	Princeton	Princeton	6	11
" 24	Syracuse	Syracuse	13	6
" 28	Ithaca	University of Pennsylvania	4	7
June 1	Philadelphia	"	1	3
" 4	Ithaca	Williams	4	8
" 11	"	Lafayette	11	8

* * *

Columbia.

Dates.	Played at	Opponents.	Columbia	Opp.
April 1	New York	Trinity School	10	5
" 2	Princeton	Princeton	3	8
" 8	New York	New York N. L.	1	17
" 13	"	New York University	13	10
" 22	"	Harvard	2	7
" 23	"	Forfeit, Princeton	9	0
" 30	"	University of Pennsylvania	0	3
May 4	"	Manhattan College	3	9
" 7	Orange	Orange A. C.	7	5
" 14	Hackensack	Orintavi F. C.	7	11
" 19	New Haven	Yale	1	23
" 21	New York	New York University	9	7

You want the best? Of course you do!
Come to us and you will get it, and at the same
time you are protected by our "year's guaran-
tee or money back!"

Our special line of black vienna thibets for
coat and vest, with a striped English trousering,
Suit to order, $20.00. Overcoat of covert cloth,
kersey or melton, silk lined, $18.00.

Samples mailed free.

ARNHEIM,

BROADWAY & 9th ST.

WE HAVE NO OTHER STORE.

Varsity Crews. Season of '95.

Cornell.

POSITION.	NAME.	CLASS.	WEIGHT.	HEIGHT.	AGE.
Stroke	F. A. Briggs	'98	138	5.06	25
7	E. J. Savage	'98	170	6.00	23
6	R. W. Beardsley	'00	150	5.11	21
5	C. S. Moore	'98	169	5.10½	21
4	T. L. Bailey	'99	169	6.00	20
3	S. W. Wakeman	'99	168	6.00	22
2	W. Bentley	'98	160	5.11½	21
Bow	W. C. Dalzell	'99	160	5.11	20
Coxswain	F. D. Colson	P. G.	112	5.06	22

Average Weight, 160½ Pounds.

Harvard.

Stroke	F. Dolyans	'98	151	5.09½	25
7	U. Biddle	'00	160	6.00	19
6	J. H. Perkins	'98	172	6.01	22
5	C. L. Harding	'00	163	5.08	19
4	F. S. Higgenson	'00	164	6.01	20
3	E. Wadsworth	'98	164	5.10	22
2	J. D. Kernan	'00	160	6.00	20
Bow	G. S. Derby	M. S.	161	5.11	24
Coxswain	G. R. Orton	P. G.	103	5.06	23

Average Weight, 163 Pounds.

Yale.

Stroke	W. B. Williams	'00	157½	5.10	19
7	I. C. Greenleaf	'99	170	6.00	19
6	F. W. Allen	'00	181	6.00	19
5	J. H. Niedicken	'00	170	6.00	21
4	F. P. Flint	'99	167	5.11	20
3	J. P. Brock	'00	183	5.10	18
2	H. P. Wrickes	'00	168	5.11	19
Bow	Payne Whitney	'98	164	5.10	22
Coxswain	I. M. L. Walton	'99	113	5.09	18

Average Weight, 170 Pounds.

Pennsylvania.

Stroke	J. P. Gardiner		153	5.09½	21
7	S. M. Weeks		165	5.11	23
6	J. N. Busch		165	6.00	22
5	L. Kintzing		154	5.10	19
4	J. B. Snover		170	5.11	22
3	L. G. Buckwalter		161	5.11	21
2	J. H. Hall		160	5.09½	21
Bow	A. H. Elickwin		161	5.10½	19
Coxswain	J. S. Wise		102	5.03	21

Average Weight, 152 Pounds.

Columbia.

Stroke	B. B. Silt		159	5.11¾	20
7	O. W. Erdel		165	6.00	20
6	J. W. Mackay		169	5.11	21
5	E. P. Shatuck		160	6.00	20
4	F. T. Jones		163	5.10	20
3	H. H. Oddie		169	6.00	21
2	C. H. Maden		153	5.08	21
Bow	A. G. Betts		161	6.00½	22
Coxswain	M. E. Boyne		102	5.03¼	17

Average Weight, 162 Pounds.

Results of Races

JUNE 23RD	NEW LONDON.		FOUR MILES.
Cornell		23 minutes	38 seconds.
Yale		24 "	2 "
Harvard		24 "	35 "

JULY 2ND	SARATOGA.		THREE MILES.
Pennsylvania		15 minutes	51½ seconds.
Cornell		16 "	6 "
Wisconsin		16 "	10 "
Columbia		16 "	21 "

⊹ New Hoffman House, ⊹

Madison Square, New York.

Absolutely Fire-Proof.

Conducted on the European Plan.

ROOMS $2.00 PER DAY AND UPWARDS.

J. P. CADDAGAN, Manager.

COLUMBIA FOOT BALL TEAM.

MAUSER M'F'G CO.,

TRADE MARK

~ SILVERSMITHS ~

Members of Committees will find it to their advantage to get
our estimate and designs for

PRIZE TROPHIES, CLASS OR FRATERNITY PINS.

A call at our show room will give ample opportunity for a selection
from our large and varied stock of Wares in
Sterling Silver.

Shop and Factory,

NO. 14 EAST 15th STREET,

N. Y. CITY.

O. B. STRONG & CO., Representatives.

Foot Ball Records of the Leading Teams for 1897.

PENNSYLVANIA.

Pennsylvania	17	Bushnell	0
Pennsylvania	35	F. and M.	0
Pennsylvania	18	W. and J.	4
Pennsylvania	57	Gettysburg	0
Pennsylvania	33	Bucknell	0
Pennsylvania	55	Lehigh	0
Pennsylvania	42	Virginia	0
Pennsylvania	34	Dartmouth	0
Pennsylvania	24	State	0
Pennsylvania	46	Lafayette	0
Pennsylvania	40	Brown	0
Pennsylvania	20	Indians	10
Pennsylvania	22	Wesleyan	0
Pennsylvania	15	Harvard	4
Pennsylvania	4	Cornell	0
Total	465	**Total**	20

YALE.

Yale	10	Trinity	0
Yale	30	Wesleyan	0
Yale	12	Amherst	0
Yale	32	Williams	0
Yale	10	Newton	0
Yale	18	Brown	14
Yale	24	Indians	9
Yale	6	West Point	6
Yale	16	Chicago	6
Yale	0	Harvard	0
Yale	6	Princeton	0
Total	170	**Total**	35

WEST POINT.

West Point	38	Trinity	0
West Point	12	Wesleyan	9
West Point	0	Harvard	10
West Point	30	Tufts	0
West Point	6	Yale	6
West Point	48	Lehigh	6
West Point	42	Brown	0
Total	176	**Total**	31

BROWN.

Brown	24	Tufts	0
Brown	44	Boston	0
Brown	20	Andover	4
Brown	24	Wesleyan	12
Brown	14	Yale	18
Brown	0	Harvard	18
Brown	0	Pennsylvania	40
Brown	24	Newton	0
Brown	18	Indians	14
Brown	0	West Point	42
Brown	12	Wesleyan	4
Total	180	**Total**	152

CARLISLE INDIANS.

Indians	0	Princeton	18
Indians	9	Yale	24
Indians	82	Gettysburg	0
Indians	10	Pennsylvania	20
Indians	14	Brown	18
Indians	23	Illinois	6
Indians	10	Cincinnati	0
Total	158	**Total**	86

THE LATEST CRAZE.

The Sweetest Love—Waltz Song.

My Dear Little Girl and I.

WORDS AND MUSIC BY
C. FLORIAN ZITTEL.

AS SUNG IN THE
LEADING THEATRES.

Order Early.

Price 50 Cents.

Music of all Publishers

❧ Supplied at Lowest Prices without Delay. ❧

Published by M. WITMARK & SONS,
N. Y. City.   Chicago.

O. B. STRONG & CO.,
258 Broadway, N. Y.

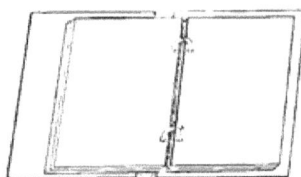

PRINCETON.

Princeton	44	Lehigh	0
Princeton	53	Rutgers	0
Princeton	28	Annapolis	0
Princeton	34	State College	0
Princeton	18	Indians	0
Princeton	54	F. and M.	0
Princeton	10	Cornell	0
Princeton	12	Elizabeth	0
Princeton	30	Dartmouth	0
Princeton	57	Lafayette	0
Princeton	0	Yale	6
Total	**340**	**Total**	**6**

HARVARD.

Harvard	20	Williams	0
Harvard	24	Bowdoin	0
Harvard	13	Dartmouth	0
Harvard	32	Amherst	0
Harvard	10	West Point	0
Harvard	24	Newton	0
Harvard	18	Brown	0
Harvard	52	Newton A. C.	0
Harvard	24	Cornell	5
Harvard	24	Wesleyan	0
Harvard	0	Yale	0
Harvard	6	Pennsylvania	15
Total	**223**	**Total**	**20**

CORNELL.

Cornell	6	Colgate	0
Cornell	16	Syracuse	0
Cornell	18	Tufts	0
Cornell	4	Lafayette	4
Cornell	0	Princeton	10
Cornell	5	Harvard	24
Cornell	45	State College	0
Cornell	42	Williams	0
Cornell	0	Pennsylvania	4
Total	**133**	**Total**	**42**

LAFAYETTE.

Lafayette	15	Bloomsburg	0
Lafayette	20	Wyoming	0
Lafayette	24	State	0
Lafayette	5	F. and M.	0
Lafayette	64	Temperance A. C.	0
Lafayette	4	Cornell	4
Lafayette	0	Pennsylvania	46
Lafayette	34	Lehigh	0
Lafayette	0	Princeton	57
Lafayette	10	Dickinson	0
Lafayette	41	Wesleyan	6
Lafayette	22	Lehigh	0
Total	**256**	**Total**	**110**

WILLIAMS.

Williams	0	Laureates	0
Williams	0	Harvard	20
Williams	0	Yale	32
Williams	0	Lehigh	5
Williams	0	Wesleyan	22
Williams	0	Colgate	18
Williams	6	Amherst	6
Williams	0	Cornell	42
Williams	0	Dartmouth	52
Total	**12**	**Total**	**197**

J. GLASSMAN.

LATE WITH JOHN PATTERSON & CO.

LADIES' TAILOR,

481 FIFTH AVENUE.   *NEW YORK CITY.*

THE PROGRESS RIDING HABIT.

Celebrated, and used by ladies of leading families throughout the United States and Europe.

The Progress Riding Habit requires no elastics, it is self-adjusting in mounting and is perfectly safe in dismounting.

I especially wish to state that the Progress Riding Habit was patented by me, November 7th, 1893, and cannot be obtained elsewhere.

ALSO SUITS, COATS, ETC.

COLUMBIA TRACK TEAM.

BARTENS & RICE CO.,

328 Fifth Avenue,

.

Formerly 20 John Street,   NEW YORK,

IMPORTERS AND MANUFACTURERS OF

Watches and Ornamental

JEWELRY.

<-->

DIAMONDS AND DIAMOND ORNAMENTS IN GREAT VARIETY
AND UNIQUE MOUNTINGS. FINE WATCHES OF ALL DIFFERENT
GRADES, SPORTING AND REPEATING WATCHES INCLUDED . . . .

<-->

Also the latest designs in Ornamental and Useful Silverware.

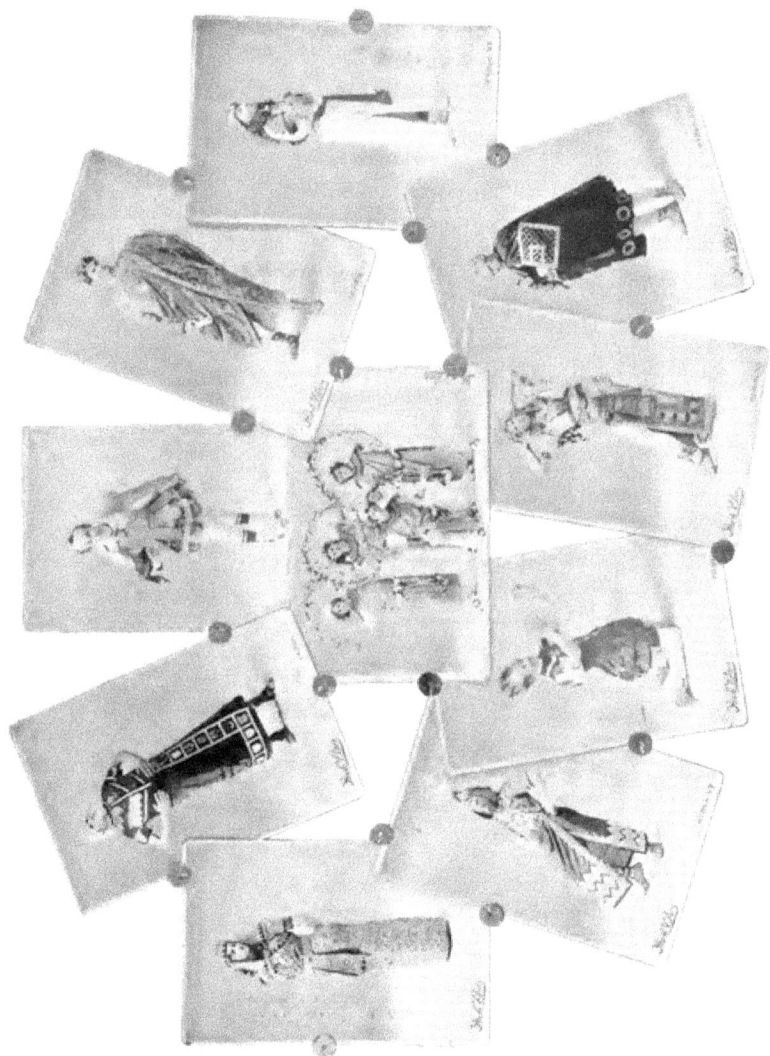

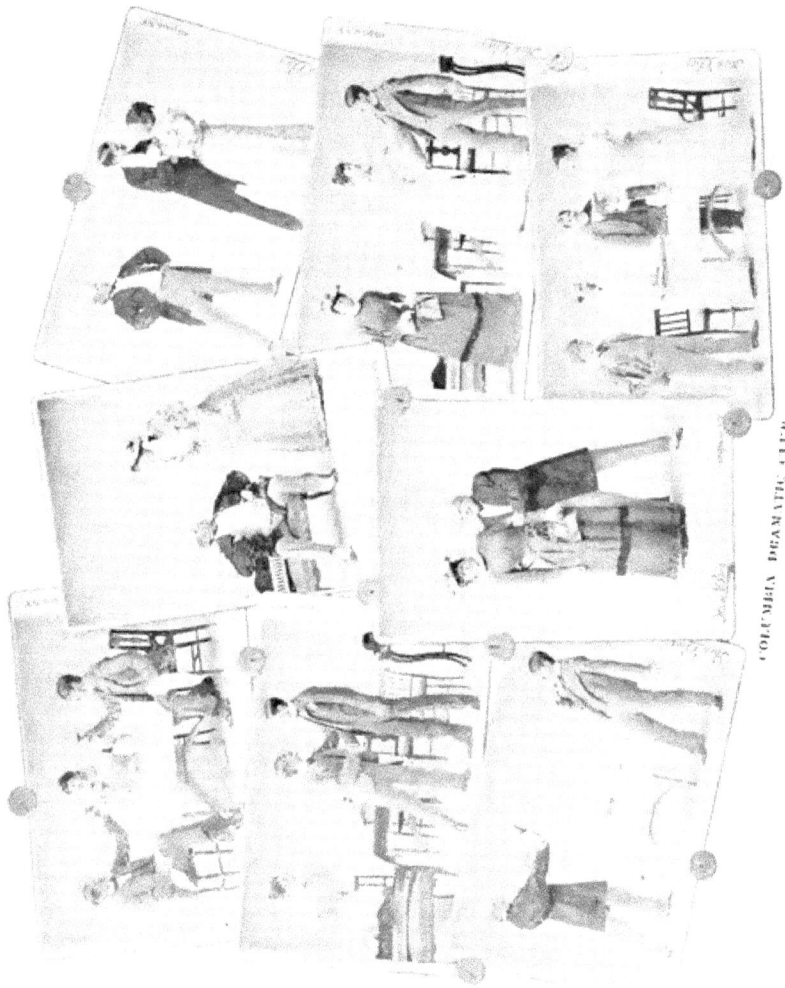

www.ingramcontent.com/pod-product-compliance
Lightning Source LLC
Chambersburg PA
CBHW031456270326
41930CB00007B/1030